The Music Factory

Keyboard Workbook 2

Christopher Wilson

A practical music course for
National Curriculum Key Stage 3/GCSE
General Editor: Jonathan Rayner

FABER 𝆑𝆑 MUSIC

Preface

To the Student

This book will help you to learn keyboards in a structured and progressive way. In addition to covering the technique of playing the instruments, the book will introduce theory in a practical manner, drawing the link between understanding, performance and invention. It is important that you follow through the materials in the given order, as each unit builds upon and develops the skills and understanding learnt in previous units.

To the Teacher

This book aims to develop technique alongside musicianship skills. It encourages students to take a creative approach to learning an instrument. A guiding principle behind **The Music Factory** has been the wish to bring about a closer overlap, exchange and cohesion between classroom and instrumental music lessons.

These books cover the earliest stages up to GCSE level, with students working either individually or in groups. The material has been planned carefully so that concepts and technique are introduced, consolidated and developed together. Musical pieces, exercises, etc. are notated using one of the following systems:

1. Standard pitch and rhythmic notation
2. Standard rhythmic notation with pitch numbers and solfa
3. Short scores — notated melodies with chord symbols
4. Graphic notation

Students should be encouraged to choose a system which suits them. The pitch number or solfa systems are particularly commended in that they emphasize the interrelationship of notes within the scale, and enable students to transpose more readily.

Every other Unit contains an ensemble piece arranged for all the instruments in this series. The scores are to be found in a separate volume, and the **Teacher Resource Book** contains additional materials which could be adapted for instrumental work.

These workbooks are designed to be used flexibly, in one or more of the following ways:

— In normal classwork under the direction of a teacher skilled in the basic techniques of each instrument.
— By one or more multi-skilled specialist instrumental teachers working with a group of similar or mixed instruments. (The Guitar and Bass Guitar books are particularly suitable for teaching alongside each other.)
— By separate specialist instrumental teachers. The method is particularly suitable for group tuition.

The authors recommend the value of specialist support, but hope that their approach will make it more cost-effective.

© Faber Music Ltd 1993
First published in 1993 by Faber Music Ltd
3 Queen Square London WC1N 3AU
Music and text set by Seton Music Graphics Ltd
Design by James Butler
Cover design by Shirley Tucker
Photographs © David Hughes unless otherwise stated
Printed in England by Caligraving Ltd
International copyright secured
All rights reserved

By the end of this unit you will have:

1 *played some semiquaver rhythms in* $\frac{4}{4}$ *time*
2 *played the natural minor scales of A, D and E*
3 *invented riffs using semiquavers in* $\frac{4}{4}$ *time*
4 *invented a counter melody to a given melody*

1 Rhythm bank

Establish a beat and clap the rhythms below:

Now play them, using one note of the keyboard, as usual.

2 The natural minor scale

Play the natural minor scale of A as shown below. Practise the right hand first, then the
left, and finally both hands together. Use the fingering indicated.

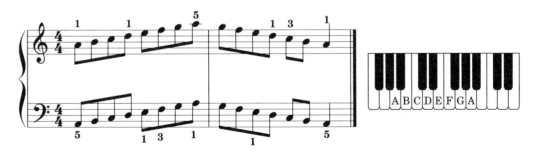

Notice that this scale consists of the minor pentatonic scale with its two 'gaps' filled in.
(The two new notes, incidentally, are the 'extra' ones needed for triads IV and VII in the
previous unit.)

Can you see how it is related to the scale of C major? The two scales have exactly the same notes, but begin in different places: the natural minor scale of A begins on the sixth note of the major scale of C.

Work out the interval between each note and the next. All the intervals should be either a tone or a semitone.

The pattern of tones and semitones this gives you is the same for every natural minor scale, no matter what note it begins on. Use it to work out the natural minor scales of E and D, each of which requires one black note.

3 The ♩♪♪♩ rhythm

Invent some *riffs* over the following chord pattern, using the ♩♪♪♩ rhythm. A *riff* is a short musical shape which keeps repeating itself. You may find it easiest to take notes from the chords themselves, though you could experiment with others as well.

Make sure your riff changes at the same time as the chord: in the first bar, for instance, you need 6 semiquavers for chord I, but 10 for chord V.

Also try an octave lower

I   V   IV   V   I

4 Inventing a counter-melody

Play the well-known Christmas carol *God rest ye merry, Gentlemen*:

Invent another treble-clef melody which fits with the tune: this is called a counter-melody. The second part should move mostly in parallel with the tune.

Here is a suggested beginning, which you could continue:

etc.

Which intervals sound best in the two parts?

5 Sight-reading

These sight-reading tests use both hands together for the first time.

Moderately fast

Slow

Slow

By the end of this unit you will have:

1 *played dotted quaver rhythms in* $\frac{4}{4}$ *time*
2 *played the natural minor scale over two octaves*
3 *used the tremolando technique to sustain notes*
4 *played the keyboard part of Ensemble Piece No.5*
5 *transposed more complex melodies*
6 *sight-read more complex melodies*

1 Dotted quaver rhythms (♪.♪)

Clap the following rhythm:

Now clap this rhythm, which is the same except for two ties:

This could be written as follows, using dots rather than ties. Remember, a dot after a note increases its length by half as much again: so a quaver with a dot after it is the same as a quaver tied to a semiquaver.

2 Rhythm bank

Establish a beat and clap the following rhythms:

Now play them, using one note of the keyboard, as usual.

3 The natural minor scale of A (2 octaves)

Play the natural minor scale of A over two octaves, as follows. As usual, practise first with the hands separately.

Repeat the scale using the dotted quaver rhythms introduced above, in this manner. Again, it might be helpful to practise first with the hands separately.

As in the last unit (Unit 10), use the tone/semitone pattern of the natural minor scale to transpose this two-octave scale into D and E. The pattern of fingering is the same as the above, though the actual notes will have changed.

Now play the following two riffs, which use rhythms from the RHYTHM BANK and the two-octave natural minor scale. The riffs are notated using pitch numbers and Tonic Solfa, so play them in all three natural minor scales you have just played — A, E and D. Note how these notations show which octave to use by means of commas. The full two-octave scale is as follows:

l, t, d r m f s l t d' r' m' f' s' l'

1, 2, ♭3, 4, 5 ♭6, ♭7, 1 2 ♭3 4 5 ♭6 ♭7 1'

In Solfa, the use of the comma changes with d, in pitch numbers with 1

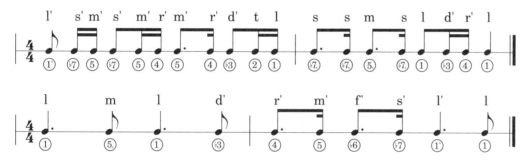

Play each of these phrases again and improvise (invent) a two-bar answering phrase.

4 Technical exercises

Technique is what we call the physical side of the ability to play a keyboard instrument.

Technical exercises are designed to develop a particular aspect of technique, sometimes more than one at once. The first of these exercises, for instance, is for a technique known as *tremolando*, which involves the rapid alternation of two or more fingers playing the same note.

Choose any white note on the keyboard and play it repeatedly with the right hand, using your second and third fingers, thus: 3 2 3 2 3 2 *etc*. Start slowly. Once your fingers are used to the alternation, stop and repeat the exercise a little faster, choosing a new (white) note if you like. You will find it easier if, instead of your fingers going simply up and down, you pull the tips towards you, as though you were 'flicking' the keys: your two fingers, in fact, should be giving an imitation of someone running on the spot.

When the right hand has mastered the technique, repeat with the left hand, using the same fingers — 3 2.

11

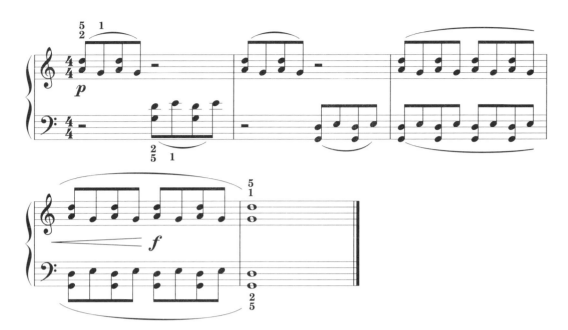

The second exercise is designed to develop a slight roll of the wrist, rather like the one you need to turn a doorknob. At the same time it makes sure that the roll is not too extravagant by including two-note chords: so take care the notes in the chords sound exactly together.

5 Dynamics

Dynamics simply means how loud something is to be played and what signs are used to indicate this. Like many terms in music, dynamics are Italian in origin.

There are six basic levels of loudness in music: you could perhaps think of them as the numbers 1–6 on the volume knob of a television or radio.

We use the initial letters of the Italian words as follows:

Volume	Sign	Italian	English
6	*ff*	fortissimo	very loud
5	*f*	forte	loud
4	*mf*	mezzo forte	loudish
3	*mp*	mezzo piano	softish
2	*p*	piano	soft
1	*pp*	pianissimo	very soft

(The full name of the piano is *pianoforte*, which, as you can see, means softloud. Unlike the harpsichord or organ, the piano will produce a soft or loud sound depending on how hard you press the key.)

When we want a passage of music to get *gradually* louder, we write the word *crescendo* (*cresc.* for short) where we want it to start getting louder: or we can mark the whole length of the increase with a crescendo sign, which looks like this: ⟨ .

For getting gradually softer, there are two words: *decrescendo* (*decresc.*) or *diminuendo* (*dim.*). The corresponding sign is: ⟩ .

6 Ensemble Piece No.5: *Pentatonic Rondo* (Jonathan Rayner)

Here are the melody and keyboard parts for *Pentatonic Rondo*. Practise each in turn carefully.

repeating pattern

repeating pattern

repeating pattern

repeating pattern

pattern ends

Team up with another keyboard player and play the piece as a duet.

Now play the piece in a multi-instrumental arrangement (drums/percussion, bass guitar, guitar and keyboard); your teacher will explain which part to play and how the piece is put together.

7 Bolivian folk song

This folk song from Bolivia has been written using pitch numbers and Tonic Solfa symbols. Choose one of the natural minor keys you know (A, E or D) and sight read the piece, ignoring the ties to begin with.

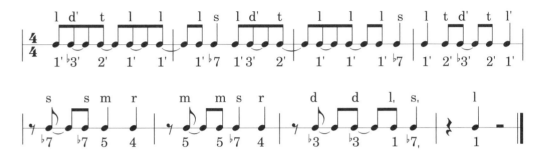

Using the same natural minor key, practise the piece until you can play it with all the ties. If you have difficulty at any point, remember to count out loud: 1 + 2 + 3 + 4 +. It sometimes helps as well to play over a tricky passage without ties first.

Once you have mastered the tune in your chosen key, play it in the other two keys.

Now *harmonise* the melody, that is, add appropriate chords underneath it. Play the melody in E minor and use chords from the following Triad Bank:

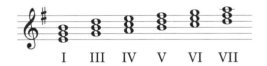

Try using only one chord per bar to begin with.

UNIT 12

By the end of this unit you will have:

1 *played some rhythms in $\frac{6}{8}$ time*
2 *transposed a piece for three players*
3 *played a triad exercise in $\frac{6}{8}$*
4 *sight-read in $\frac{6}{8}$ time*

1 Six-eight time ($\frac{6}{8}$)

Remind yourself of the opening of Unit 4, where you learned how to count quavers. Repeat the same exercise, tapping crotchets with your foot and clapping quavers, but this time use $\frac{2}{4}$ time, as follows:

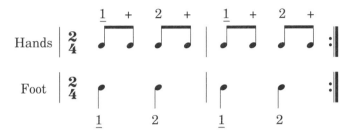

Sometimes, though, we divide each beat into *three*. Repeat the exercise, with your foot tapping at exactly the same speed, but this time clap *three* times for each tap of the foot.

If you have difficulty, think of the opening of the song *Oh dear, what can the matter be?* The words 'Oh dear' give you the speed for your foot to tap, while the words 'what can the matter be' show you how fast to clap your hands.

When we write music like this down, we still use quavers for the quicker, clapped notes. But because there are now three quavers to every beat, a crotchet is not long enough. We need a note that lasts three quavers, in fact we need a dotted crotchet.

That is $\frac{6}{8}$ time: two beats in a bar, each a dotted crotchet, which can be split into three quavers. The tapping/clapping you have just done, written in $\frac{6}{8}$ time, looks like this:

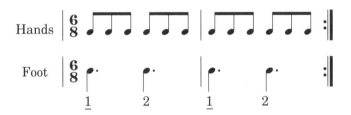

When counting $\frac{6}{8}$ out loud, some people say '$\underline{1}$ and-a $\underline{2}$ and-a', while others use '$\underline{1}$ 2 3 $\underline{2}$ 2 3'. Decide which you find the easier, and use that.

For a beat's rest in $\frac{6}{8}$ some people dot a crotchet rest ($\xi\cdot$), but more use two rest signs, a crotchet and a quaver ($\xi\gamma$).

2 Rhythm bank

Establish a beat in $\frac{6}{8}$ time and clap these rhythms. You may notice that pattern A is the one used by the opening of *Oh dear, what can the matter be?*

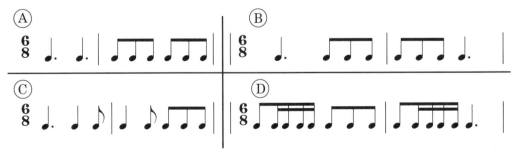

Now play these rhythms on one note, as usual. You could use the *tremolando* fingering learnt in the previous unit, if you like.

Notice how, in $\frac{6}{8}$ time, quavers and semiquavers have their tails joined together in groups adding up to a beat, such as: ♩♪♪ ♪♫♪ ♪♬

3 Piece for three players

Below you will find the opening tune of *Morning* (from Grieg's music for the play *Peer Gynt*) arranged for three keyboards. But before you get together with two other players, there is some preparation you need to do by yourself.

First, revise the C major scale you learned in Unit 6.

Now transpose this major scale into E, the same way you transposed it into G and F in Units 6 and 7. (Hint: E major needs four sharps — in fact, it has more black notes than white)

Practise the following four-bar piece, playing through each of the three parts in turn. Grieg's original tune is in the middle part. Then play through the three parts of the separate section marked '4a'.

Key: C major
Moderately fast

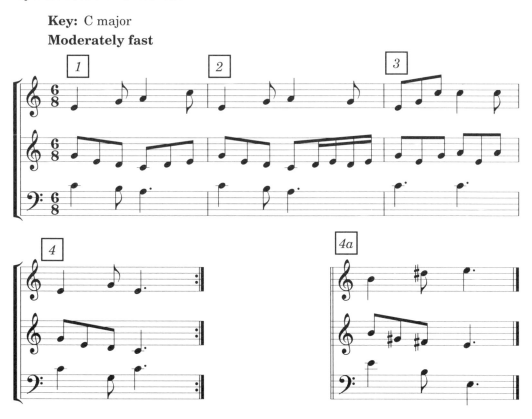

Now repeat all three parts of the piece, transposed into E major. You should find the top line begins with a G♯, the middle line a B and the bass an E.

When all this is secure, you are ready to play the piece with others.

Team up with another two keyboard players. Decide which of you will start with which of the three parts. Play through bars 1–4 several times in C major, swapping parts each time. Repeat in E major.

Finally, play through the piece four times in a row, twice in C major and twice in E major. The second time through in C major, replace bar 4 with bar 4a: it makes a better 'join'.

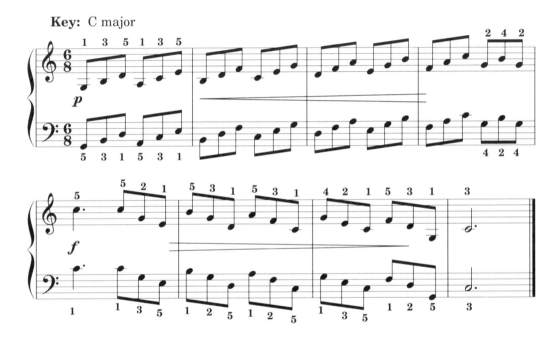

This should give you the following 16-bar piece:

bars 1–4 in C major
bars 1–3 in C major, plus bar 4a
bars 1–4 in E major
bars 1–4 in E major again

Each player should keep to the same part for the whole 16 bars, but then swap over and repeat.

4 Triad exercise in $\frac{6}{8}$ time

Play the following triad exercise, paying careful attention to the fingering and dynamics. You may find it helpful to practise first with the hands separately.

Key: C major

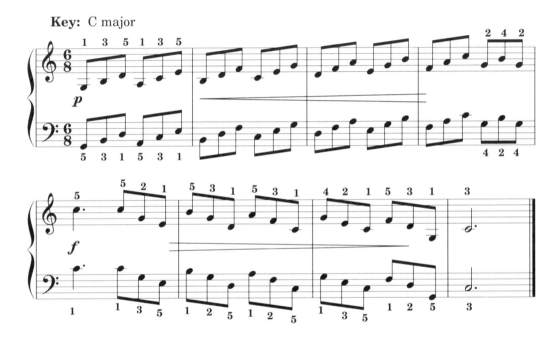

Notice in the last bar that the dotted minim (𝅗𝅥.) is used to fill a bar of $\frac{6}{8}$ as well as a bar of $\frac{3}{4}$.

6 Sight-reading in $\frac{6}{8}$ time

Here are two more advanced pieces of sight-reading, using the natural minor scale and $\frac{6}{8}$ time. In both cases the right hand has the main melodic idea, while the left has an accompanying role: most keyboard music is this way round.

At the end of the first piece are the words '*poco rit.*'. These are in Italian. *Rit.* is short for *ritardando* or *ritenuto*, both of which mean 'getting gradually slower'. For the opposite, speeding up, we use the word *accelerando* (*accel.* for short). *Poco* means 'a little', so *poco rit.* means 'slow down a little'.

Key: E minor
Moderately slow

Key: D minor
Very Slow

By the end of this unit you will have:

1 *played various rhythms in* $^{12}_{8}$ *time*
2 *played a dominant 7th chord*
3 *played through some common chord progressions, including a 12-bar blues*
4 *played a blues shuffle with guitar, bass guitar and drums*

1 $^{12}_{8}$ Time

$^{12}_{8}$ is like $^{6}_{8}$, but with four beats in the bar instead of two. Use your hands and one foot to clap and tap this pattern, as you did in the previous unit:

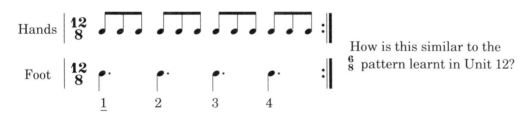

How is this similar to the $^{6}_{8}$ pattern learnt in Unit 12?

Times such as $^{12}_{8}$ and $^{6}_{8}$, where beats are sub-divided into three rather than two, are called *compound times*.

13

2 Rhythm bank

Establish a dotted crotchet beat and clap the following rhythms in $\frac{12}{8}$ time:

Now play them on your keyboard, using one note.

3 Common chord progressions

Revise the G major scale learnt in Unit 6. Play it over two octaves using rhythms from the RHYTHM BANK above.

Build triads on the 1st, 2nd, 4th, 5th and 6th notes of the scale, as follows:

Take triad V and add an extra note to it, a seventh up from the root:

Chord V (whatever the key) has a special name, the *dominant*, and the new chord, with the added seventh, is called the *dominant seventh*.

Play the following two sequences of chords. Play the root notes in the left hand and all the notes (including the root again) in the right hand. Reposition the notes of the right hand chords so as to minimise movement of the hand, as in Unit 9. Play both sequences in C, G and F majors.

| I | VI | II | V⁷ |
| I | VI | IV | V⁷ |

A sequence of chords like these is called a *chord progression*. Many well-known pop/rock songs have used these very progressions. For instance Buddy Holly's *Every Day*, Ben E. King's *Stand by Me*, Lennon & McCartney's *This Boy* and so on.

4 The 12-bar blues

Another common chord progression is the 12-bar blues, the basic structure of which is:

$$\begin{smallmatrix}12\\8\end{smallmatrix}\quad \text{I} \;/\;/\;/\;|\;\text{I}\;/\;/\;/\;|\;\text{I}\;/\;/\;/\;|\;\text{I}\;/\;/\;/\;|$$

$$\text{IV}\;/\;/\;/\;|\;\text{IV}\;/\;/\;/\;|\;\text{I}\;/\;/\;/\;|\;\text{I}\;/\;/\;/\;|$$

$$\text{V}^7\;/\;/\;/\;|\;\text{IV}\;/\;/\;/\;|\;\text{I}\;/\;/\;/\;|\;\text{I}\;/\;/\;/\;|$$

The 12-bar blues progression lies at the base of much jazz and pop music. There are many refinements and variants, some of which are will be covered later, but this is the pattern in its simplest form.

Play the 12-bar blues in C major in $\begin{smallmatrix}12\\8\end{smallmatrix}$ time: the root notes in the left hand in dotted crotchets, and the chords in the right hand twice as slowly, in dotted minims. Repeat in G major and F major.

Revise the minor pentatonic scale, learnt in Unit 8, and play it starting on G: the notes are G, B♭, C, D and F.

Team up with another keyboard player. One of you play the 12-bar blues, as above, in G major; the other improvise a solo using the notes of G minor pentatonic. Then swap over parts.

Here are some ideas to help you with the improvised solo:

1 Start simply, using only a few notes.
2 Don't be afraid to make full use of any rhythmic ideas you have: a repeated rhythmic idea, even if it uses only one or two notes, can sound very exciting.
3 Use as much of the pitch range of your keyboard as you like, so long as you only use the notes of the G minor pentatonic scale.
4 Vary the dynamics (don't play your solo all loud or all soft).
5 Use a range of different sounds (*timbres*): try to make some notes sound crisp, others full and juicy, others like the chime of a bell, and so on.

5 Ensemble Piece No.6: *Shuffle the Blues* (Richard Beard)

Here are the melody, harmony and bass parts for *Shuffle the Blues*, which takes the form of a 12-bar shuffle. Practise each in turn carefully.

Team up two other keyboard players and play the whole piece as a trio. Repeat, swapping parts.

Once the piece can be played as written without much trouble, the player taking the melody line (printed on the top) could replace this with an improvised solo using the notes of the C minor pentatonic scale: C, E♭, F, G and B♭.

Now play the piece in a multi-instrumental arrangement (drums/percussion, bass guitar, guitar and keyboard); your teacher will explain which part to play and how the piece is put together.

6 Sight-reading

These pieces both use $\frac{12}{8}$ time. Make sure you pay attention to the dynamic markings (*mp*, *f* etc.) and the 'tempo indications' — the words that tell you how fast to play.

UNIT **14**

By the end of this unit you will have:

1 *read rhythms in various time signatures*
2 *decorated a melodic line*
3 *developed your knowledge of the dominant seventh chord*
4 *harmonised a melody*

14

1 Rhythm bank

Establish a beat and clap the following rhythms. Use the same speed of beat despite the change of time signatures.

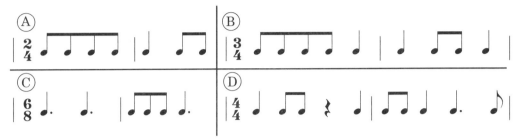

Now play the rhythms on your keyboard, using just one note as usual.

2 Melodic decorations

Simple melodies can be 'filled out' to make the line more interesting and decorative. Read and play the following examples. Notice how notes are added at each step, making the tune more elaborate.

Use the same sort of technique to decorate these two melodic lines:

Now try decorating the tune of *God rest ye merry, Gentlemen* from Unit 10.

3 The dominant 7th chord (V⁷)

Unit 13 showed the formation of a dominant 7th chord.

Here the chord is split between the hands: the left hand has the root while the right hand has the remaining three notes. This *four-part harmony*, as it is called, has also been used for chord I, so one of the notes has had to be 'doubled'. Which is it?

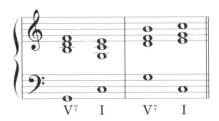

Play this short example in hymn-tune style. Notice at the end how the chord V⁷ helps to push the music to its close: the 7th in the chord of V⁷ falls to the 3rd of I, while the 3rd of V⁷ rises to the root of I, as shown by the arrows.

Compare the V⁷ – I at the end with the V – I a bar earlier. V⁷ – I is much stronger and more final.

4 Harmonising a melody

Here is the theme from the slow movement of the *New World* Symphony by Dvořák. You played the first eight bars of it as a duet for two players in Unit 5.

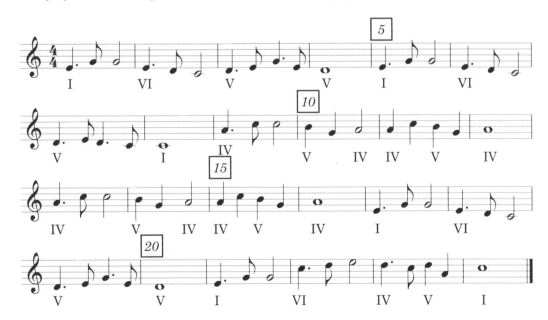

Harmonise the tune according to the chord symbols which have been added. As well as the melody line at the top and chords in the middle, you will need a bass line underneath. Make sure that the bass line uses one of the notes belonging to the chord, but where possible make your bass line move in the opposite direction to the tune. (In music, moving in opposite directions is known as movement in *contrary motion*).

5 Five-finger walking exercise

This exercise is designed to get your fingers used to different-sized intervals. Every bar uses the same fingering, but the intervals change.

In the second bar all the notes are a semitone apart — movement like this is called *chromatic*. Chromatic melodies contain accidental signs — a new sign, the natural ♮. The natural is used to cancel either a sharp or a flat. (All accidentals remain valid for the remainder of the bar in which they occur, unless cancelled.) This exercise uses a natural in the second bar:

15 UNIT

By the end of this unit you will have:

1 *played triplet rhythms*
2 *played the keyboard piece of another ensemble piece*
3 *sight-read a piece involving triplet rhythms*

1 Scales

Play over all the scales you have learned so far.

2 Quaver triplets

Sometimes in simple time, such as $\frac{2}{4}$ or $\frac{3}{4}$, a composer wants to divide a crotchet beat into three instead of two — just as if it were a beat of $\frac{6}{8}$. In such cases we simply write three quavers with their tails joined together and show they are to be played in the time of two quavers by writing a figure *3* under or over the middle quaver, like this:

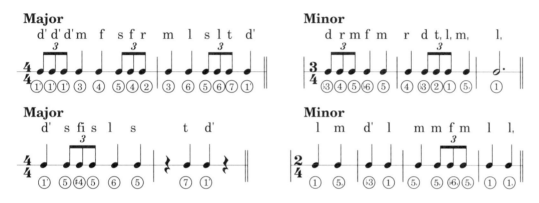

Some people also use a tie to bracket the three notes together.

Play through these melodies which contain quaver triplets. One at least should be very familiar to you! The melodies have been notated using pitch numbers and Tonic Solfa, so play them in as many different keys as you can.

Major

Minor

Major

Minor

3 Ensemble Piece No.7: *Ballet*
(arr. Jonathan Rayner)

Here are the melody, harmony and bass parts for *Ensemble Piece No.7*, which is taken from a collection by an early 17th-century German composer called Praetorius. Practise each part in turn carefully.

Notice that the piece consists of two eight-bar phrases, each of which is followed by a decorated repeat.

Team up with two other keyboard players and play the piece as a trio. It could also be played as a duet: player 1 has the melody part in octaves, while player 2 takes the harmony part in the right hand and bass part in the left hand.

Then play the piece in a multi-instrumental arrangement (drums/percussion, bass guitar, guitar and keyboard); your teacher will explain which part to play and how the piece is put together.

Da Capo

4 Sight-reading

16 UNIT

By the end of this unit you will have:

1 *split a* $\frac{3}{4}$ *rhythm between the hands*
2 *played the scales of D and B$\flat$ majors*
3 *harmonised a melody using major 7th chords*
4 *improvised on a given rhythm*

1 Coordination exercise in $\frac{3}{4}$ time

In the following exercise a single rhythm is split between the hands: the hands take one note each in strict alternation. To begin with, practise the rhythm by tapping the hands on any surface, such as a table top:

Note that the exercise begins on an upbeat. Because we have created an extra beat with this upbeat, it is normal in written music to shorten the final bar by one beat, so that the piece adds up to a whole number of bars. In this exercise the crotchet upbeat, added to the minim at the end, makes a whole bar.

Now play the rhythm on the keyboard, using a D major triad in the right hand and a D in the left:

Notice (in the right hand) that only the first F of each bar needs a ♯ sign in front of it.

Any sharps, flats or naturals that are *not* part of a key signature are called *accidentals*, as though they were something that shouldn't have happened. Accidentals affect the note they precede and any other on the same line (or in the same space) for the remainder of the bar.

Because an accidental is only valid for one bar, it has to be repeated when it is still needed in another bar, as it is here.

2 Scales of D major and B♭ major

Remind yourself of how you transposed the major scale into G and F in Units 6 and 7. Work out what the notes should be in the major scales starting on D and on B♭.

When you have found the right notes, play the scales, with hands separately, over two octaves. See if you can work out how the scales are best fingered (Hint: in scales thumbs are never used for black notes.). The correct fingering is given at the end of this unit for you to compare.

Practise the two scales (still hands separately) with the correct fingering until you can do them from memory. Then put the hands together.

3 Harmonising a melody using 7th chords

The melody you are about to tackle is in D major. To begin with, here are triads built on each note of a D major scale.

Play them.

I	II	III	IV	V	VI	VII
maj	min	min	maj	maj	min	dim

In each case the triad has been described by its type. You should have already played major and minor triads in Unit 8. Triad VII is probably 'new' to you: it is known as a *diminished triad* as it consists of two intervals of a minor third. It looks rather like a dominant 7th chord that has lost its root:

16

VII   V⁷

and in harmony is almost always used as such.

7th chords can be built on any note of the scale, not just the fifth. Here are 7th chords on each degree of the scale. Play them.

maj7   min7   min7   maj7   dom7   min7   min7♭5

The chords keep the major/minor qualities of the simple triads above. The 7th chords built on the first and fourth notes of a major scale have a special kind of sound. These chords are known as major 7th chords because the 7th note is only a semitone away from the root note: the notes of Dmaj⁷ are D, F♯, A and C♯.

In the case of all other 7th chords built on the major scale, the 7th is called a minor 7th, being a *tone* away from the root: the notes of an A⁷ chord are A, C♯, E and G.

Notice that chord VII is described as ♭5, meaning the chord has a flattened fifth.

The harmony of the following melody by the French composer Erik Satie contains both major 7th and minor 7th chords. Major 7th chords are used at the beginning to create a special 'floating' atmosphere.

In the last few lines, Satie uses bass notes which do not belong to the chord being used. To show this, the bass note is separated from the chord symbol by an oblique stroke.

The piece is repeated, but the second time the ending is slightly different. This is shown in music by the use of a *first-time bar* and *second-time bar*. When you play the piece for the first time, you play all the music beneath the bracket marked ⌐1. . When you get to the repeat sign, you play the piece again from the beginning; but this time you *omit* all the music marked with the ⌐1.   and, instead, carry on from the passage marked ⌐2. , immediately after the repeat sign.

Play the melody first and then the chords.

Then play the piece as a duet with another student, one of you playing the chords, and the other the melody.

When you have produced your version, try to find a recording or the music of this beautiful piece and listen to Satie's original.

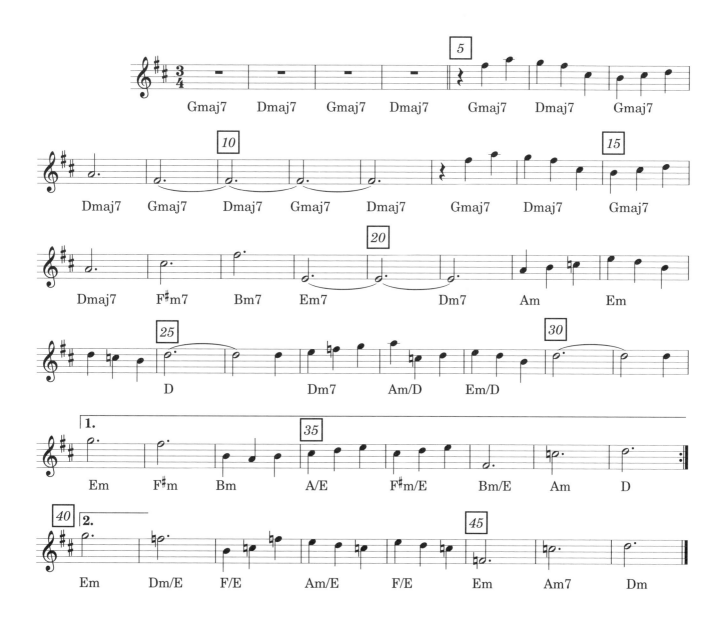

4 Improvisation on a set rhythm

Improvise a piece based entirely on the rhythm used at the beginning of this unit:

The following hints should help you:

1 *Clap the rhythm through until you are completely familiar with it.*
2 *Choose a sensible speed that suits the rhythm and the way you see it.*
3 *Don't keep repeating the rhythm without any modification or variation, or the piece will turn out very monotonous.*
4 *But don't change the rhythm so much that it is unrecognisable, or the piece will lose its way and become confused.*
5 *Try to give your piece some framework apart from being based on one rhythm. For instance, you could come back every so often to the notes you used with the rhythm right at the very beginning.*
6 *Return to the given form of the rhythm at the end, to give a 'rounded off' feel.*

Here is an example of how the rhythm could be made the basis of a 16-bar improvisation. It starts with the given rhythm, followed by two variations, and ends with a repeat of the given rhythm.

Notice how the tied figure used in bars 1 and 3 of the given rhythm has been made a focus for the improvisation.

5 Extra study

Here is the fingering for the major scales of D and B♭:

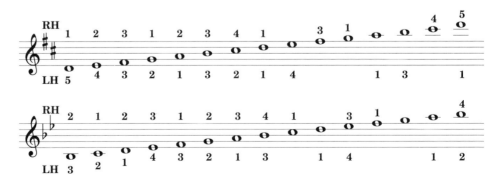

and here are the 7th chords belonging to those scales:

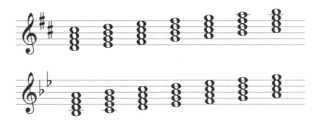

Work out corresponding 7th chords for the major scales of C, F and G.

The Burt Bacharach/Hal David classic *This guy's in love with you* features 7th chords.

As an extension to the improvisation exercise above, try to make up a set of theme and variations. Begin with a simple tune like *Oh, when the saints*, then produce variations on it, each variation altering the melody and rhythm in a particular way. Make sure each variation has the same number of bars as the original tune.

UNIT 17

By the end of this unit you will have:

1 *played coordination exercises in $\frac{4}{4}$ and $\frac{6}{8}$*
2 *played in the Mixolydian mode*
3 *played a 4-3 suspension*
4 *played triads in the 1st inversion*
5 *taken part in an ensemble piece using the Mixolydian mode*
6 *sight-read some more complex rhythms*

1 Coordination exercises

Here are two more exercises like the one in Unit 16 where a single rhythm is split between the two hands. As before, first tap out the rhythms with the hands on any convenient surface, then play it with the given notes.

The first example is in B♭ major: the right hand has the triad of that key and the left hand the root.

The second example is in D major and uses a 7th chord, with the upper three notes in the right hand and the root again in the left:

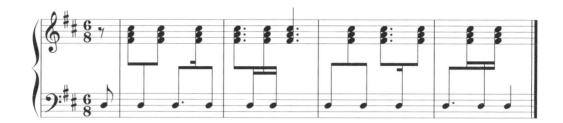

Both examples ($\frac{4}{4}$ and $\frac{6}{8}$) begin with a quaver upbeat. In the $\frac{6}{8}$ example this extra quaver can be balanced by shaving a quaver off the end of the final bar: if you count, you will see it contains only five quavers' worth of notes.

But in the $\frac{4}{4}$ example this is not possible, since the final quaver is needed for a note. In such cases, the upbeat often becomes a whole bar, with the unused portion filled with rests, as here.

2 The Mixolydian mode

Not all music uses the major/minor harmony system, with the dominant chord 'directing' the harmony. Music in the middle ages used scale patterns called 'modes', traces of which still persist in some traditional folk music. These traces were borrowed by folk-influenced pop singers and in this way have made their way into pop itself.

This scale is called the *Mixolydian Mode*:

This is rather like a scale of C major, but starting and ending on G. Work out what the notes of the *Mixolydian mode* would be, beginning on C, then on D and finally A. What major scales share the same notes as these, in the same way that C major shares its notes with the *Mixolydian mode* on G?

The only difference between the *Mixolydian mode* on G and the scale of G major is the seventh note, which is lower in the mode than in the major scale. It is this lowered seventh that is so characteristic of folk music, such as this example:

Play this tune, then join up with a few other players (either keyboard or guitar/bass guitar). Working as a group, invent for the tune a suitable chord progression and bass line. Note that in the Mixolydian mode, V is a *minor* chord. Perform your arrangement, making any adjustments that seem necessary.

3 The 4–3 suspension

The *4–3 suspension* is a simple and effective way of decorating a triad or chord and is common in popular music. In a 4-3 suspension, the 3rd of the chord or triad is temporarily replaced by the 4th note up from the root.

Here are examples in C major and C minor:

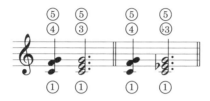

Notice how the 'clash' between the 4th and 5th notes (F and G) creates tension which is released when the 4th moves to the third. The movement is known as the *resolution* of the suspension: the chord has *resolved*.

In the examples above, the whole chord was repeated with the resolution, but it is more common for just the 4-3 to move:

The chords can be repositioned to put the 4-3 at the bottom or top, depending on the effect required. Compare the following:

Here is a short example in B♭ major which applies the 4-3 suspension to chords I, II, V and I again:

4 The first inversion

A chord or triad is said to be in the *first inversion*, or to be a *first-inversion chord/triad*, when it has the 3rd rather than the root at the bottom.

Here, for instance, are triads on every degree of the scale of B♭ major, written in first inversion:

With chords, the important note is the one in the bass. In the following example, the right hand triads change a great deal, but the bass note in the left hand does not. All the chords to the left of the double bar (with B♭ in the left hand) are root-position chords: all those to the right of the double bar (with D in the left hand) are *first-inversion* chords.

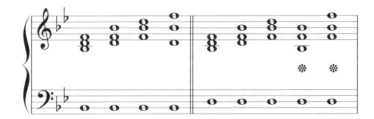

Notice that in the two first-inversion chords marked *, the 3rd (D) has been omitted from the right hand: when you compare them to the preceding three chords, you will find first-inversion chords sound better if you *don't* double the 3rd.

You have already used inversions in earlier units, to make sequences of triads in the right hand smoother and easier to play. Inversions are also much used to make bass lines smoother and more melodic.

Compare the effect of the two versions of the same progression which follow. The first has every chord in root position (with the root in the bass), and all the triads in the right hand are arranged in root position. In the second version, the second chord has used the first inversion both to vary the sound of two B♭ chords together and to make the bass line slightly more melodic: the right hand triads, too, have been inverted to reduce hand movement.

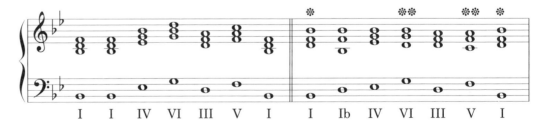

I I IV VI III V I   I Ib IV VI III V I

The first version is awkward and 'jumpy' compared to the second.

The chord marked 'Ib' is the only *genuine* first-inversion chord in this example: the 'b' after the chord number is the proper sign for 'first inversion'. Even though all the other chords are in root position, you can still speak of the right-hand triad-shapes marked '*' as using the first- inversion.

The triads marked **, as you may probably have guessed, are called 'second inversion triads'. These are dealt with properly in Unit 21.

Play the chord progression I IV II V III VI V I in the following ways, keeping three notes in the right hand and one in the left:

1 root-position chords throughout, with right-hand triad-shapes all in root position
2 root-position chords throughout, with right-hand triad-shapes inverted for smoothness
3 root-position and first-inversion chords, right-hand triad-shapes inverted for smoothness.

5 Ensemble Piece No.8: *Mixolydian Theme and Variations* (Eric Richards)

Here are the melody, harmony and bass parts for *Ensemble Piece No.8*, a theme and variations using the Mixolydian mode on G. Practise each part in turn carefully.

Team up with other keyboard players and play the whole piece together as a keyboard trio. Swap parts as appropriate.

Now play the piece in a multi-instrumental arrangement (drums/percussion, bass guitar, guitar and keyboard); your teacher will explain which part to play and how the piece is put together.

17 6 Sight-reading

These two sight-reading exercises use the rhythms from the beginning of this unit. The first of them is based on the scale of D major, and you can use the same fingering as the scale.